# SEVEN BOXES FOR THE COUNTRY AFTER

Wick Poetry Chapbook Series Five
Catherine Wing, Editor

# SEVEN BOXES FOR THE

# COUNTRY AFTER

*Poems by Janet McAdams*

*The Kent State University Press*
*Kent, Ohio*

**Ohio Arts Council**
A STATE AGENCY
THAT SUPPORTS PUBLIC
PROGRAMS IN THE ARTS

Library of Congress Catalog Card Number 2015040837
ISBN 978-1-60635-296-0
Manufactured in the United States of America

The Wick Poetry Series is sponsored in part by the Wick Poetry Center at Kent State University.

Library of Congress Cataloging-in-Publication Data
Names: McAdams, Janet, 1957- author.
Title: Seven boxes for the country after : poems / by Janet McAdams.
Description: Kent, Ohio : The Kent State University Press, [2016] | Series: Wick Poetry
    Chapbook Series ; 5
Identifiers: LCCN 2015040837 (print) | LCCN 2015041050 (ebook) | ISBN 9781606352960
    (pbk.) ∞ | ISBN 9781631012389 (ePUB) | ISBN 9781631012396 (ePDF)
Classification: LCC PS3563.C263 A6 2016 (print) | LCC PS3563.C263 (ebook) | DDC
    813/.54--dc23
LC record available at http://lccn.loc.gov/2015040837

# CONTENTS

# ACKNOWLEDGMENTS

Poems from this collection have appeared previously in *Sentence, VerbSap,* and as part of a 40th Anniversary online feature at the *Black Warrior Review.*

Many thanks to Lesley Wheeler for her suggestions on an earlier version of this manuscript.

When we thought to leave the house of the country, the country after fever, the land liened and lost, I bundled the twelve pages, the first for the life we led. Another to list the lies the body remembers: two eyes and a tongue, the pink chords of the voice box, the hand that points or gestures or copies it down like this: 1 2 3. Three pages for relatives unfaced and sad as watches. One for the names never spoken. One to fold into a box the size of a head. One torn to pieces, small enough to be carried by wind or water. One for ash, two twisted to light the oily kindling. The last, this one, this page you are reading.

Note:

tear on page 4 through the words *cut, carry, remember;* ink smeared in 3rd paragraph of page 622 [N.B. check with printer about insoluble ink, about solvents, about liquids the body produces]; page 7, index, missing in 3rd & 4th printings: the letters *g-h,* beginning with '*gut,*' up to but not including '*head,*' as in *here is where he put his head down* or *that is when she realized it at a gut level* or, {variation}, *we have gutted the treasury* or *the new hunters have gutted a doe;* pages of 7th signature have been restitched with twine waxed & tired of being licked; pages of 4th signature starting to unbind.

They are loading the people onto buses. They are loading them onto flatboats. There is a girl with a broken hand. A man with a cane and a box tied with cord. Skin cracking and leaking something other than water. Stone, lilac at the edges, curls toward water. If they could lie down and dream about the long forest of childhood, clover juice, the acorn cup brimming with rain, a berry bright as blood, bright as a crayon. The dream where no knife parts skin, not even the surgeon's. Where nothing peels, not the life wrinkled around them, or fruit too green and sour to burst against their hands, beneath their thick-soled feet.

We saved words in a plastic box with a lid, the kind people used when they had food left over, but those words took on the scent of peaches or fried meat until one by one they ~~meant~~ ~~read only~~ said: *the past*. You kept a few rolled in a piece of brown cloth, but they blurred in the winter damp, until every letter became a blue face or the silhouette of an animal, the kind we hardly ever glimpsed at the edge of the city. Some words, closed in a jar like fireflies, blinked then went out. Some we mistook for lozenges and sucked on them when our throats were raw. A few—*hurry* or *hammer* or *love*—were white with fat and had to be swallowed whole. A day will come when only the clouds can spell: horse-lying-down or woman-with-her-arms-outstretched. Night will fall before they float into boys or dogs or a stack of hay. When one curls into *C* or reminds us of *L*.

Stranger, list the ways weather tilts the body forward, from the ice body to the body made of sand, the body called from mud. The way weather passes through cell by cell, along spine or synapse. How it runs down the body's current, the long route past lightning or storm. Pay attention to the way a hand curls, how the tendons of the neck tighten, the skin's memory of shock and spark. Because you are no stranger to blood or muscle, the bones that refuse to settle, the legs that kick when the body falls toward darkness and comes back to fall again. Stranger, sleep has its own technologies. It lets you walk through snow or walls or water. It lets you linger in that other country. Do you remember? It tugs like a dry wind, that day the body refused to lie down.

You need to bear down with the heel of your hand to start the heart beating. You need to breathe into the quiet mouth, to halt the bright blood spurting, yet let it flow from any wound made by nail or claw, tooth or talon. You need to lean into weather when it is wind or water, to tear through longing's thin sheath, the plastic covering the pill to cure pain, the oily wrapper around fish or fry-up. Here are three candles to light the body's winter. Here is a cracked map and a broken-legged chair you can prop on a slab of marble. Lie down only when you are sure it is over. Your tongue? Hold it. Catch your breath, whisper. Lie down after weather, after the body's storm is over. Stilled tongue, stilled mouth, stilled finger, and now the red fire fading—how quiet once the hum is over. How after everything in the still air.

Left the broken tools, after the farm is auctioned, the tune the fathers used to whistle. Left a toy, a shoe, a scrap of paper blown from hand or bin. Left a bone, the smaller half of the split wishbone, left the wish not taken. Left over, the cold meat, the weeping pie. Left the direction a wave breaks when seen from shore, the side where you part your hair, the ring hand that says I chose or settled. Left to turn, left to leave the state, right to love it. Left alone, left behind, left or leaving by blade to throat or razor to wrist, mouth to gas, lung to water. Left the hand belonging to the devil, the hand forced to lie fallow in lap or table. Left behind, the ones who could not see God. Left the door you go into when the right one is locked. Left or left, the heart after they burned the fields, after we stopped counting steps or miles. Left the side of the heart that calls the blood back from the body.

*If* white is the color of mischief, then these white walls, this little house of marble we hide behind, willing the man with his notebook to find someone else to follow. We hide, kin to bone, to tuft of fur caught in the chain-link fence, to everything under the snow: tooth, grass, a skunk's belly bloated and facing heaven. *If* earth, then ground and the body it blanketed. *If* winter, then salt to eat the rubber from your boots, to sting skin already cracked and weeping. Skin, that blue edge between weather and the bodies we used to carry. Didn't we hope something else might rise from the snow and rock us to sleep? Rock us long past the dreaming of what we had lost.

When will they call? What will you tell them? Can you remember? How many were there? Who led and who followed? Is this your notebook? Do you take notes? What did you write down? How many did you influence? Where did you lie? Where do you sleep? Did you have meat for dinner, a good life, a thick enough blanket? Point to the place where your skin is tender. Do you hate to be alone? Do you love your family? Who are your relatives? Where did you get that scar? Do you recognize this photograph? Who is the child in the photograph, the woman in the blue dress? Were those shoes expensive? How well do you sleep? Do lights move across your window at night? Do you check the street for unfamiliar cars? Do you have all your teeth? Did you know that fish can breathe underwater? How many bones are there? How many, in the human body?

He photographed the letter you were writing. He dusted the doorknobs for prints, gathered up: nail parings, skin that sloughed off in our sleep, the black hair from my comb, the brown from your wooden-handled brush. He recorded the sound of us holding our breath, measured the temperature of palms, counted the silence between heartbeats, gathered the sweat from foreheads, from upper lips, from armpits. He wrote us down, in black ink, in writing we could not read. He wrote us down in a notebook with a pencil he sharpened between sentences. We shrank from the light of his torch. We shrank in the lens of his camera. By the time his black car pulled away from the curb, we were small enough for the pocket of his briefcase.

They said: *Confess.* But the body was too in love with its own skin. It wept a yellow shadow of water from pore and finger. How it wanted a bed of green leaves for lying. How it wanted a silver sky over and no holes or openings. Confess, they said, confess. She said: I shaved my hair rather than see it fall to age or poison. She said: I buried the books. I burned the shopping lists and valentines. I lanced and cauterized. Don't listen for my father's story, my mother's voice. Only watch for the way words hover in the air between us. I have what you need but nothing you've asked for. Don't wait for me to call out, to name your gods, to whisper the hiding places of citizens or soldiers.

That you had loved butter and chocolate. That salt could not cure every illness. The words backpack, better, back then, bury. Your dream about the leafed-up world. A box half the length of your body. The god you turned from, his palms threaded with metal. What must fold or arch. The slubbed ends of toes, tips of fingers. What aches now and what in time will refuse to straighten. The science of nails, how to make pegs to hold a table together, a solid enough surface for bowls of stew, a dress to mend, sums divided, subtracted, and forms to fill out and sign and send. The page torn but pieced back together. The joke you made that someone overheard. The look on your face when everyone else was singing.

No, it is impossible. You cannot dream for five minutes. You must go down into the valley of rapid eye, of legs thick with paralysis. You must go down, so far down, to come back. We woke you from safety. You couldn't stay there. We had to wake you and wake you. You couldn't. You cannot. You cannot stay. Say goodbye to the field of berries, the day you picked them with your sister. Say goodbye to the city you flew over, floating with a boy you loved in high school. Floating a blue cloud. A place by a shining river. Say goodbye to the Dream Animal, with its sweetly human face, its body furred with white. How it rocks you in a thick pelt of lap while you sing your tired song. But say goodbye. Goodbye! Goodbye! You cannot stay there. We need you, in a small room, beneath a clear, white light, to tell us. We need you to tell us.

*Come closer,* she whispers from the doorway. *Come,* she holds a finger to her lips, *You may have my story for a coin, a loaf of bread, a promise to whisper. There was a country,* she begins, her voice low as cities forgotten beneath the water. We look away, we are ready for travel. *No,* she says, *not like that,* begins again: *Once upon a time in a country. . . . No, no—In the country of* _____ *&* _____. *In the country of Remember, of Rock and Sand, of Silence and Blue Ash. Say you remember.* We shake our heads. No. No, we say. We turn, we see the parting in the trees. *Come back,* she calls. *Come back for the rest of the story.* No, no, we say. Not today, we can never remember.

We said: If the fires come closer, we'll have no choice except leaving. We thought of skin just burned or skin, red hot, cinnamon on the tongue. We remembered the lie that the doctor's needle will not burn, the lie of beginning again: the trunk of old letters cast out to sea surfacing a mile away, a few yards away, the length of an oar, the length of an arm. The hands that reach to pull it to shore, then cast it back, thick as a rope of morning, night tied down and anchored by light so white it blues around the edges like the overcooked yolk of an egg. You could not swallow the meat we had, the tongue of an animal, cat or rabbit, pink as my burned hands. Pain ran up my arms in waves so fierce I wondered what it was like to be tortured.

We passed through a village holding its Festival of Weeping. The villagers cried in steel buckets and brought their tears to the cauldron boiling in the square. They slurped down round bowls of sorrow, except the children who cried even harder remembering bread with jam, candy canes sucked to sharp points after Christmas. For the pot, there were tough little onions left over from winter. Some greens, a carrot, a cup of milk. And sweat from heat, from decades of labor. The postmistress threw in a string of blue beads she'd had since childhood. The mayor one damp wool glove. And the baker a wooden spoon with a broken handle. One voice complained, 'This soup is too salty,' and the river roared up for a moment and stretched a swollen finger toward the pot. The soup grew plain, sweeter than plain, and when we left, every thirst was quenched, every hunger.

First in a life the rice body, the food body, the body made of meat, the body of drift and slow turnings. The first body had to go on sleeping. The first body had to slurp and gobble. It had to shit into a porcelain bowl of water. It had to snore like a sow. It had to wipe the green snot from its face. It had to bleed onto cloth or paper. It had to sweat its fevers into the sour linen of a mattress of feathers and foam. That body went and came. Later you had to learn the body that coughed and whispered. The body that sighed and lifted. That unfolded cells. How its blue blood turned red. How it rose and fell, like a kite learning each layer of unasked for weather.

Here is a bowl of water, a clean cloth, a whisper. Wash the first story, lie to the second, send the third off to school where it will learn to play with other children. Here are drawers, wooden baskets, boxes. Take this key. Put this key in your pocket. Hold this key so tight the teeth cut into skin. Here is a blanket for folding or spreading or spreading over. A canvas tarp in case of rain. A knife to scratch directions in the ground. Soon morning will crack the green cold with light, and lies run from your ears, from your mouth, from your fingers. Here are dry twigs, pages, matches. Write what never happened.

Seven boxes for the country after. Box of wild green: the color of sour apple, dull bruise, blades of grass, each plucked against the heat of what we used to call summer. The saltbox, the one that leaked white all over. The lick deer came to in winter. The sea where anything will float and the water, they say, blind you. Box of hard edges, of knife blade, glass. Of wince, shirk, and the fear of being found out. Of needle and pierce, crack and cut. Box of body or thumb, the one held out to drivers or sucked years after childhood. The box of that god who is always tired on Fridays. So hope he decides to leave work early, that yours is not the life planned out when he is bored or lonely. But inside the seventh are bones and muscles, a set of directions. A map unfolded and the last box opened, full of cloud, mist, fog. Wish for wind or sun, something to blow or burn it all away.

Watch the silver circle of time, the hands moving, the way water laps the floating body. Watch the one with too much luggage, the one with a blue knapsack, the one who carries nothing. Watch the one who looks hungry, the one with thick glasses. Watch for webbed fingers, tongue tucked between teeth, head unhooded. The marked wrist or shoulder, skin shadowed by fence or doorway. The watch: Yours, curfew to dawn. Mine, the shift after. Watch every exit. Watch for looking or writing. For counting. Watch the way weeks give themselves to months, the way years turn to stories, each blue square of window grated against looking, every door closed to telling. Watch the one who looks at the ground. Watch the sky for change. Watch for words reappearing.

When the blue water changed to blue flowers and there was nothing to drink but yellow pollen licked from face or finger, how you floated in bluebells. How I gathered sea holly, a swatch of scotch thistle for the antique merchant who dusted off a globe of the old new world. How we had only the papers we had bought from someone leaving. That we had forgotten where to stand or lie down, en route to the country longed for. How we circle or don't circle, or hover, or crick our necks looking back or looking elsewhere. Off the Coast of Remember, someone is swimming against the undertow. We hold our breath hoping he will drown or be saved soon. Anything to have it over.

Not yet the years worked down to sand. Or earth, packed and paved, longing to shift or breathe. Not yet soil, broken and tilled, sprouting to green. Not still the motion of scrape, of grind. The moment of hands, cupping. The moment that called skin cells to linger. For sweat to salt the nooks and crannies. Not now in the dead breath of building. In the kingdom of drawer and false light. Why not just rise through clay, through sand? The layers that learned us, then shifted away. Think of the god we could turn to. The hand that might find us. A voice to know and name us. From there the world leans closer, not away.

At one of the stations we came to, a girl jumped from the train for a cola, leaving her notebook on the table, her jacket on the back of the chair. Weeping, she chased the train when we left her. We were just then crossing the border between Never and Not-Like-This. For fifty miles, I watched the space she once occupied. Until the engineer wiped his face with the sleeve of her jacket. Until the student tore a page from the notebook to write the address of a coffee shop he wanted to visit. We passed a field with a scarecrow, unshorn sheep, a village so poor they licked salt from each other's faces. A family got on at the crossing and sat down at her table, pushing aside the few molecules of her breath that lingered. In the pension's green hallway, I climbed up a flight of stairs that narrowed and narrowed until it disappeared. I marked this point *X*, with the pencil I took from her satchel.

We undress behind a screen in a small room in the space between countries. They search our pockets, tossing it all in a box marked THINGS, half full with false teeth, a tangled wig, a book losing the old skin of its binding. They search our folds, our stories, peeling away wrist scars, the doctor's thumbprint on a vein in my neck, from the year I tried to sleep all winter. Calluses rubbed by bad shoes, a hangnail, a false tooth, the twisted veins of your ropey arms. They take: our shoes, our pockets, the hole from the lobe of your left ear, the skin that sifts like snow in cold weather. They take until we are tender as babies, until we have nothing left to declare.